LINKED
BY THE
JOY OF WORDS

BY

LESLIE MOISE

R. C. Linnell Publishing

Linked by the Joy of Words

ISBN-10: 0996148108

ISBN-13: 978-0-9961-481-0-8

Cover art and design by Eve Forbes.

Published by:
R. C. Linnell Publishing
Louisville, KY 40205
www.LinnellPublishing.com

Other Books by Leslie Moise:
Judith (ISBN: 978-1-59719-075-6)
Love is the Thread (ISBN:978-1-59719-048-0)

Author contact information:
LeslieMoise@gmail.com

Dedicated

to

the memory

of

Beverly Giammara

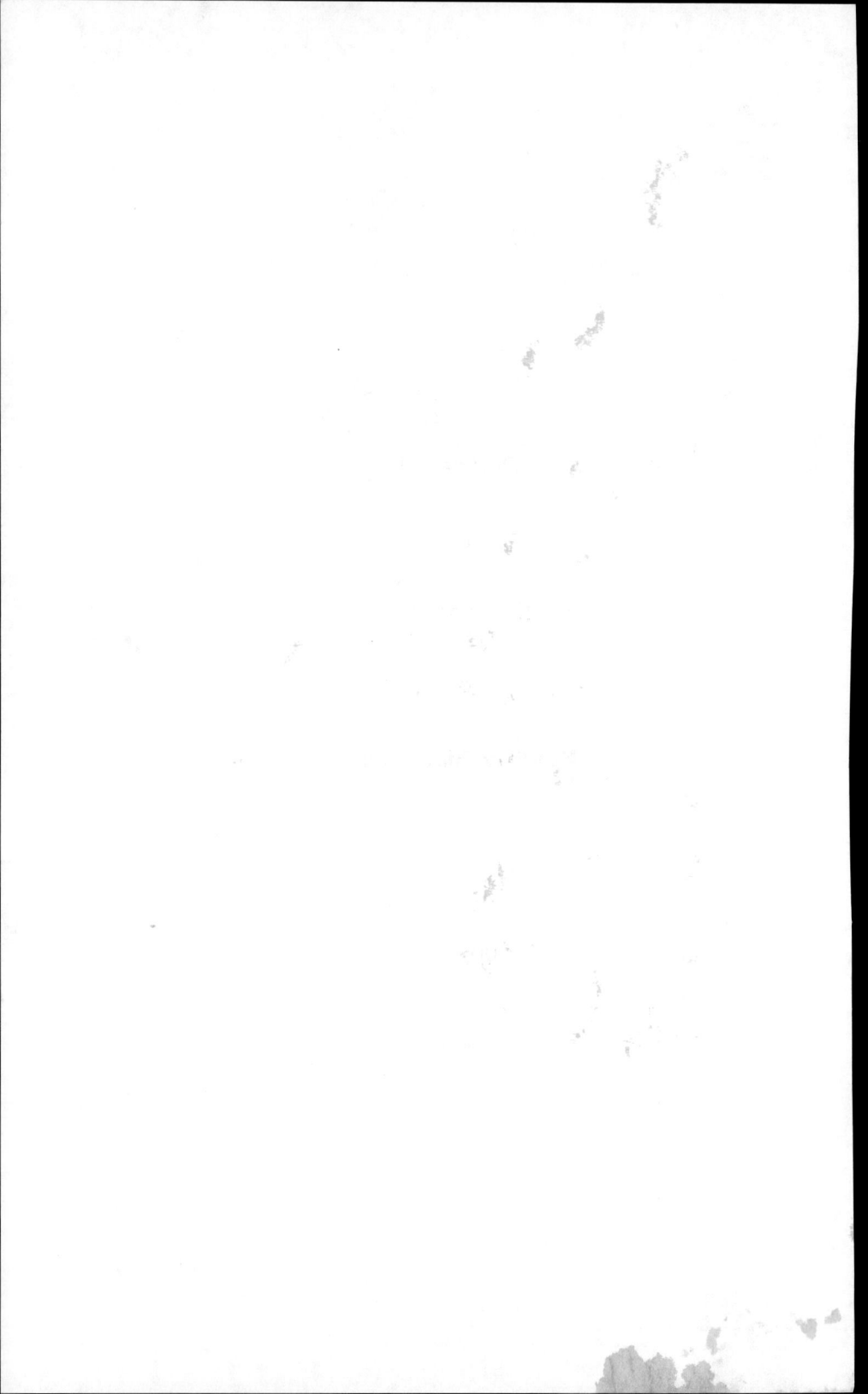

ACKNOWLEDGMENTS

Thanks to Cheri Powell for making the dream of this book a reality. My heartfelt gratitude to Eve Forbes for putting so much effort and creative vision into the cover and art. Thanks to JJ Haws for his ongoing tech support and being such a good man. Blessings to Paschal Baute for his guidance and friendship, and to Patricia West for her friendship and support.

Beverly Giammara was one of the rare individuals who can truly be called a Renaissance Woman. Her interests, talents and accomplishments ranged from the scientific to the poetic. Passionate about learning, her formal education overlapped that of her three sons. When her eldest graduated from high school, Beverly completed her undergraduate degree. She completed her Master's degree at the same time her youngest graduated from high school. Beverly accomplished all of this while working a full time job. Her lifelong drive and quest for knowledge inspired her sons, who all graduated from college.

After she came across the electron microscope, her life was never the same. She published technical papers, received patents, won awards, and was considered an expert electron microscopist. One of her most publicized projects was an evaluation of Zachary Taylor's remains to determine if he had been poisoned.

What made Beverly unique among scientists was her equal talents in the arts. She painted beautifully; learned metal etching, decoupage, candle making and was an ardent photographer. Her rich singing voice was discovered early, and she sang at her sister's wedding. Later, Beverly regularly performed with The Pride of

Kentucky chorus. She belonged to a number of writers groups, wrote thousands of poems and drafted two novels. Beverly had nearly completed the second at the time of her death in August, 2014.

Alongside her own multi-talents, Beverly excelled at recognizing other people's gifts. Generous with her knowledge and praise, she encouraged other artists to excel and stretch. She died with grace and graciousness, and a number of her friends have commented about what she taught them in the last months of her life.

INTRODUCTION

Beverly Giammara and I were friends for almost three decades. We met in a writers group, but writing poems and fiction served as only part of the foundation for our friendship.

In the nearly thirty years we knew each other, we shared many different interests and experiences. We went to the movies and theater, visited bookstores, thrift shops, and attended lectures and readings as well as book signings. Sometimes we would just be totally silly together.

A few weeks before Beverly died, someone asked her what she thought was the meaning of life. She answered at once. "To make friends and keep them."

In these pages I celebrate the years of our friendship and grieve her loss. I hope you grow to know and love her as much as the many people fortunate enough to have called her friend.

6

LINKED BY THE JOY OF WORDS

Beverly was president
of the first writer's
group I joined.
She intimidated me:
her taut hair, her authority,
the depth of her knowledge.

I found another member
more approachable.

Years later
Beverly told me she
gave the deciding vote
for my membership.
That other writer
tried to vote me down.

All the times Beverly and I
visited Goodwill.
Explored the shoes,
the videos and books,
the housewares.
Maybe found a treasure—
a blue glass vase,
a pair of sandals,
a sparkly bracelet—
to take home.

The times we
explored second-hand stores.
Designer boots.
Gowns we couldn't afford
anywhere else.

Then there's the time we
put on all the necklaces
Beverly inherited from her mother—
gold, beads, jewels—
and pranced
before the big mirrors
in Beverly's dining room.

The time she fought
to keep her job.
I couldn't do much.
Hold her hand and say,
"I believe in you."

All the times we took expeditions
to new-to-us restaurants:
A place with a reputation
for wonderful bread.
A barbecue joint.
Beverly loved
the fried dill pickles.
A small deli
with unusual sandwiches
and chocolate cake.
Half-inch creamy frosting.

Another time Beverly took me
to lunch on my birthday.
Mexican.
Already the cancer
worked inside her.
She took most of her food home.
"I'll eat it tomorrow."

Once Beverly videotaped
her writing time,
showed me
the recording later.
Herself popping up
to answer the phone
over and over.
"I don't write.
I talk on the damn phone."

She wrote thousands
of poems—
improbable verses
that paralleled her electron
microscope work
with natural images.

She wrote poetry
illustrating
her love of books,
about snow on trees
in her backyard,
a toy in the trash.
She drafted two novels.

The times
we visited the theater.
Big or shoe-string
productions.
Beverly loved them all.
Could name directors
and choreographers
all over town
and decades back.

9

Right before
her diagnosis,
she fell asleep.
Later asked
how I liked the play.
Said she didn't.

She loved
to tell the story
about her time on
"What's My Line."
How they didn't
guess what she did.
How could they?
Back then
most scientists
were men.

How she rode
to the hotel
in a limousine
with Kitty Carlisle
and the other regulars.

Beverly spent her girlhood
in Kansas.
Loved "Somewhere
Over the Rainbow."

Every time I jot down
who brought what
to writer's group,
attend a writing conference,
I think of my friend.

Each time I visit
a thrift store,
the theater, a restaurant,
or see a rainbow
Beverly stands at my shoulder.
Still in my life
linked by the joy of words,
the play of light
in water vapor
or a bargain found.

ZACHARY TAYLOR'S BONES

A biographer studied his last days,
believed political rivals
poisoned the president
with arsenic.
Authorities exhumed him.
With her electron microscope
Beverly agreed to test his hair,
bones, fingernails.
Negative results.

She thought she read
the analysis incorrectly.
Did it four times more
before she realized
Taylor had no arsenic
in him.

PRIDE OF KENTUCKY CHORUS

For the first
decades of our friendship
Beverly wore
her black hair
braided in a coronet,
the hair on her scalp
flattened
like black paint.

Then she
joined a chorus.
Loved blending
her deep voice
with theirs.
After her
first rehearsal
the ladies
gathered
around her.
"Do something
different
with your hair."

Beverly's hair
stayed in its braid.
But gradually
silvered wisps and waves
rippled around her brow.

WRITERS GROUPS

Louisville Writers Club.
The group where we
became friends.
Every other Wednesday
at Masterson's.
The group met
in empty conference rooms
in the restaurant basement,
always adjourned
to the dining room
for a late meal.
Talked about contests
we wanted to enter.
Editors who rejected
our work.
A poem accepted.

My brief sojourn
in the Chartreuse Table.
The poetry group
met every week.
Beverly attended
faithfully
for years.
Often dashed
off a poem
right before
she slammed
out the front door.
Back then,
once a week
was too much
for me.

The Friday Night Group.
Beverly invited me
to join them
at Reader's Corner.
The bookstore
made space for us
for years.

Up front in their
St. Matthews
location.
At a table
wedged
in the back room
now they've
moved to Clifton.

Writers Groups—
the stout thread
woven through
my thirty years
with Beverly.
The warp
to the woof
of everything else
we did.

BOOK SIGNINGS

Beverly and I went
to more than I can count.
I remember three
in particular.

The mystery writer
with local connections.
Gracious.
She took a few minutes
to chat with each person
in line. Hundreds of us.

She gave
a talk next day.
Beverly and I
went to hear her.
"Two days in a row.
It's a little like
a writer's conference,"
Beverly said.

The famous literary figure,
tall, thin, chilly,
who barely acknowledged
with flickering glances
that anyone
stood on the other side
of the table
stacked with books.

The also famous
suspense author.
He talked about

his writing process,
but more,
the writing process.

Every writer there
felt welcomed.
Included.
Equal.

Beverly turned to me,
whispered,
"Now you know
how to behave
when you're famous."

MY DRIVEWAY

I live in a house
partway
down a hill,
road on the crest
above the house.
The driveway leads
steeply down.
Beverly refused
to risk her
red car
to the slope.
Parked on the street,
hiked down
and walked
up with me,
arm in arm.

WHEN I WAS 27

I complained to Beverly,
"I always get
carded in bars."

One dark brow raised.
"When you're forty
you'll get on your knees

and thank God
you look so young.
I never thought
I was cute.

When I see pictures
of myself at your age
I realize
I was adorable.

Appreciate yourself
while you can."

ONE LUNCHTIME

We drove past
a restaurant.
Years before,
I lunched there
with someone who
later betrayed me.
I mentioned it
to Beverly.

She wheeled
into the lot.
Inside,
she ordered tea,
told me about a play
she just saw,
where her chorus
would travel next.

At last I joined in,
interested in what she said
instead of my memories.

Now I pass
that restaurant
and see a place
where Beverly
and I went
together.

HOW SHE MET SAM

Beverly often told me
how she met
her second husband.
Each time
I learned more.
Here is the story
I quilted together
over the years:

They met at a restaurant
owned by mutual friends.
She ate there
every week.
A professional gambler,
Sam worked there
when his money grew thin.

He asked her out.
He made a pass.
She told him
"You go to hell."

One night
months later
she dropped by
their friend's place
for a late dinner.
Sam was in a booth
with a bleached blonde
in tight jeans
and scanty top.

There's that jerk.
Beverly slid into
a booth herself.
Minutes later
Sam crossed to her.
"Say the word.
I'll ditch the bimbo,
and eat with you instead."

She stared over the
top edge of her book.
"Why?"

He leaned in,
met her stare
straight on.
"We've wasted enough
of our lives together."

Years after his death,
she still listed
Sam's name
with hers
in the phone book.

THE DRESS FORM

In the corner of Beverly's bedroom
lived a dress form. She changed
its costume every month or so.
Balanced a hat on its neck sometimes.

When I asked about it, she laughed.
Told me that after her move to Kentucky
she decided to make a dress form
since she couldn't afford to buy one.

She puzzled over how to do it
for weeks. Then she bought
enough plaster of Paris to cover
her torso. Chose a weekend

when her sons stayed with friends.
Stripped to old underwear,
plastered her body from neck
to mid-thigh, shoulders to elbows.

While the plaster heated about her,
Beverly jigged in place. "This will
be great. I can patent this idea.
Sell broke women dress form kits."

While she planned what to do
with the millions she would earn,
the plaster set. She reached for scissors
left ready on the kitchen table.

Wait—she couldn't bend her arms
to cut herself free. Now what?
She stood there. Couldn't sit.
Couldn't bend her legs.

At last she shuffled to the wall-
mount phone to call for help.
Couldn't reach the receiver. What to do?
Go outside? Scream?

"Men broke in. Plaster of Parised
my whole body so I was helpless." No, no.
Beverly didn't know her neighbors,
but she didn't want to lie to them.

She could drive downtown
to University Hospital. She knew
lots of ER doctors there. They could saw
her out and wouldn't tease her. Much.

Beverly picked up her keys, her purse,
opened the front door. Oh. The stairs
down to the walk. She couldn't bend her legs.
Couldn't sit in her car even if she reached it.

She couldn't even slam the door to vent
her feelings. What to do? Fall backward
and hope the plaster broke? She stood
in her lonely kitchen a long time.

A knock on the front door.
Beverly shuffled toward the sound
as fast as she could. *Please.*
Wait until I get to you.

On the porch stood a friend
who lived out of state. A friend
who only visited once every five
years. When Beverly opened the door

his eyes grew huge. His mouth dropped.
"What the hell happened to you?"
"I'll tell you over dinner. My treat.
After you cut me out of this thing."

MOVIES

She would call
mid-afternoon.
"Want to sneak out?"
I never asked
who we were
sneaking from.
Mostly we saw
independent films.
Only one time
did we watch
something scary.
After,
Beverly confessed
she was grateful
for the sunlight
when we left.

WHO SHE WAS

Weeks after the hospital
sent her home,
she dressed.
With a son
on each side
to steady her
she tottered
down the steps,
climbed in the car.
She wouldn't be here
for the election.
But she was here today
for the primaries.
"I'm ready to vote."

HER DOWNSTAIRS BATHROOM

Scarlet carpet.
Bright pink towels.
A claw foot tub
with its toenails
painted scarlet.

Plain eggshell walls
crowded with art,
all water themed.
The central picture?

A view of a woman's
bare legs and feet
seen from above
with the curve of a toilet seat
between her knees.

THE KIND OF THING SHE DID

Beverly tilted
her sleek head.
"Do you have
author photos?"

My mouth gaped.
"I don't have
a publisher yet."

"An author photo
will make it real."
She picked up
her bag,
saggy with cameras
and rolls of film.
"Cave Hill Cemetery
has interesting
gravestones."

I hesitated.
"Won't that look weird?'

"You write mysteries.
It'll look great."
All morning,
she shot roll after
roll of film.

I made anxious comment.
Beverly laughed.
"Photographers
take hundreds
of photos

to get one
they like."

Years passed.
I started
writing novels.
Stopped writing
mysteries.
Gained weight.
Aged.
I still have
the photo
she took that day.

CHOICE

Each of Beverly's sisters
succumbed to Alzheimer's.

Worse than anything,
Beverly feared
that sinking
into blankness.

Forgetting
all she knew.
Her friends.
Who she was.

"I won't
die
from Alzheimer's."

Less than a year later
cancer took her.

She remembered
everything
to the end.

IN HER LAST DAYS

Her sons removed
the dining table
where one of them
used to drop his peas
down the hollow metal legs.
They set up
a hospital bed.
When friends visited
she'd call out,
"I'm in here,
beneath the
chandelier."

That last month,
she had no breath.
Nothing to spare.
Asked friends
"Stay.
Chat.
I can.
Hear.
You."

THE LITERARY SALON

Visits to Beverly's
during her last months
always coincided
with other visitors.
Four. Five. Six.

Usually
other writers.
Poets.
Novelists.
Playwrights.

"Your home
is a literary salon,"
I said soon
after Beverly
came home
from the hospital.

Her eyebrows
arched high.
She grinned.
"Yeah!"

HOMAGE

She painted
at least one
self-portrait.
Other painters
made her
their subject.

Words were
her breath.
Her sons printed
a selection
of her poems
weeks
before she died.

A half dozen poets
wrote poems
about Beverly.
How she looked.
What she did.
How she died.
In the words
and images
she inspired
Beverly blooms
always.

AT THE WATER TOWER

In the same two-story room
where I got the call
that my friend
Kristine had died
of breast cancer,
more than one hundred
people gathered to celebrate
Beverly's life
and mourn her
passing.

The chorus she loved
stood before us
to sing two of Beverly's
favorite songs.

A friend who knew her well
spoke of her zest
for the arts—singing,
writing poetry and fiction,
the three writer's groups
she belonged to.
Painting. Photography.
How she loved
going to the theater.
Education.
The science she
made a successful,
decades-long career.
The three sons
she raised
into kind men.

And friends.
You only had to look
around the airy room
to see how much friends
meant to Beverly,
and she to us.
While the river
flowed silver
below the tall windows
we remembered her.
How she changed
and blessed our lives.

And for me
the extra texture:
The loss of two
friends framed
by this sunny space.

THE COUNTLESS WAYS

Beverly lived the arts.
Seeing the world's details.
Sharing what she saw
in paint or photography.
She told me how to recognize
serious photographers.
"They carry their cameras
in one hand.
Only poseurs
wear theirs on neck straps."

Once she arrived
where she wanted to shoot,
Beverly carried hers
half-hidden at one hip.
Ready to use.

She wrote poems
about life's big
and little moments:
walks down her alley,
the Twin Towers fall,
Kennedy's train stop,
ice on her front walk,
a rabbit's death.

She sang.
Four part harmony.
Traveled with the chorus
who became another family.

She created characters.
A girl, her friend, and a fort.
A scientist in the lab.

Beverly knew that life well.
The hum of machinery.
Examining insects,
bones, soft body tissues
in section.
Preparing slides,
papers, patents
presentations.

All the artists
she encouraged.
Poets she steered
to the right publisher.
Novelists she wrote with,
asked about their work.

Plays and films she saw.
Museums, art shows visited.
None too obscure.
Book conferences
she helped organize.

Weeks before she died
Beverly smiled.
"I've lived a good life,
haven't I?"

Yes.

BOOTS

When I was younger
there were people
I thought were my friends.

People who wouldn't
drive to my house
"Because it's too far."

People who expected
me to drive
to their houses,
who didn't care
that the distance
came out the same.

People who picked
fights with me
when disaster struck
in my life.

People who made
excuses
or just disappeared.

Maybe they feared
lightning would strike
them too.

Beverly drove me
forty miles
out of town
to buy snow boots
when I had none
that icy winter.

Neither of us
knew the little detail
of how to
reach the store
by back roads.

I knew the express route,
but Beverly
disliked highways.

We got lost.
Had to ask directions.
Twice.

The first time
they sent us wrong.
Tangled us in country roads
worse than ever.

An errand
we thought
would take two hours
lasted all day.

Beverly and I enjoyed
the country scenes
scrolling past.

We snacked on treats
from gas stations.
We talked
non-stop
as always.

Now those boots
don't just leave
rubber imprints
in the snow.
They spell her name
with every step.

FOR YEARS IT PUZZLED ME

She carried her camera
everywhere. Always.
Held low at her hip
ready to shoot any image
that struck her.

A church steeple
at the instant pigeons
whistled into the sky.
A slant of shadow.
A tombstone.
A friend's face.

She wrote poetry
often in the half hour
before writers group.

About the fog of dry ice
roiling through her lab.
About a statue at the museum.
Trash dumped in the alley
behind her house.

Poetry.
Photography.
How could she do
two such different things
with equal focus?

One day it struck me.
Both arts
capture a moment.
For years she used
both to say:
This is what I saw.

EVERY TUESDAY

For three months
our friend Susan
and I drove to
Beverly's
to sit by her
hospital bed.

She perched taller
against the
tilted back
when we came in,
leaned toward us.
"Tell me what's new."

In the world,
she meant.
In our lives.

Those last two Tuesdays
both times we arrived
to find her asleep.

"She's having a bad day,"
whispered
the Hospice worker.

Beverly had said
to wake her.
"Doesn't matter.
All I do is sleep."

But those last two weeks
we hadn't the heart
to disturb her.

As I left her home
for the last time
I blew her a kiss
goodbye.

A GOOD DEATH

In the three months between
the hospital
and her death,
Beverly lived as fully
as the restraints
of her hospital bed,
her converted dining room,
the ground floor of her house,
and the constant presence
of a Hospice caretaker
allowed her to live.
Beyond what most
would find possible.

She planned to write.
Soon blurry vision
and her hands refusing
to do what she wanted
defeated that dream.
Many people would have used
visits from friends as
opportunity to complain.
Not Beverly.

Except for once stating,
"I'm going to die, you know,"
she focused on visitor's lives,
their news.
She watched public television,
kept up, as always,
with the global stage
and spoke from informed perspective
about the coming primaries,

the progress of the big bridge,
with her dozens of visitors.

She did the work she could.
Wrote her will. Planned her memorial.
Where she wanted it held.
The catering. She chose foods
from our Southern culture.
Decided on the music.

Did she wish she could be there
for her big send off?
She planned a small party
a month before she died.
Just a few friends -
not so many we'd exhaust her.
Brought our favorite finger foods
and, if we liked,
something we'd written.
"Not about me,"
Beverly said as firmly
as breathlessness allowed.

We gathered in her living room,
Beverly seated at our center.
We ate zesty tomato sandwiches.
Cheese and specialty crackers.
Chocolate.
So many good things
I can't recall them all.
Some guests brought pieces to read.
A short, funny play.
Beverly laughed in
all the right places.
A homily on peace.

She bowed her head.
Nodded.
A found poem.
She offered suggestions
for a more specific title.

Toward dusk
Beverly faded.
People drifted out
in tactful ones or twos.

After the party,
after she died,
a friend spoke
about Beverly's
good death.
"I hope I die
with as much grace
as she did."

OTHER BOOKS BY LESLIE MOISE

In the ancient Middle East a pious, wealthy young widow risks her life to save her town from a besieging army. Based on the apocryphal Book of Judith.

Judith was an International Book Awards Finalist.

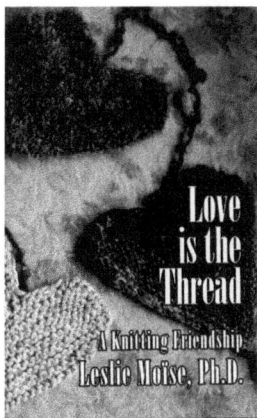

From the discovery of hidden colors in fresh snow to the satisfaction of creating a first knitted garment, *Love is the Thread* savors life's small glories, ultimate challenges, and all the moments of humor and tenderness in between.
Love is the Thread traces the way one spiritual friendship can change everything.

Available on
BarnesandNoble.com
Pearlsong.com
Amazon .com

www.ingramcontent.com/pod-product-compliance
Lightning Source LLC
Chambersburg PA
CBHW060541030426
42337CB00021B/4371